The Life of a
GEISHA

Rob Waring, *Series Editor*

HEINLE
CENGAGE Learning

Australia • Brazil • Japan • Korea • Mexico • Singapore • Spain • United Kingdom • United States

Words to Know

This story takes place in the country of Japan. It takes place in the city of Kyoto [kioutou].

 A **Old and New.** Read the paragraph. Then match each word with the correct definition.

Kyoto is a busy place with modern buildings and an ancient heart. Here you can find *kabuki* [kəbuki] theater and other artistic reminders of Japan's past. In certain parts of the city, one may be lucky enough to see a mysterious geisha [geɪʃə]. In Kyoto, these icons of old Japan can often be found walking down the street wearing *kimonos* [kəmounou]. To see one of these extraordinary women is to see a living symbol of an older Japan within a modern city.

1. *kabuki* _____

2. geisha _____

3. icon _____

4. kimono _____

5. extraordinary _____

a. a type of traditional Japanese clothing

b. a special type of Japanese woman who has learned traditional arts

c. very unusual or special; not average

d. a traditional form of Japanese theater

e. a symbol of a set of beliefs or way of life

B Becoming a Geisha. Read the definitions. Then complete the paragraph with the correct forms of the words in **bold**.

discipline: the ability to completely control the mind and body
strict: demanding; expecting rules to be followed
master *(verb)*: become an expert at something
apprentice: one who is learning a skill or trade from an expert
retired: no longer working at a job for money

A young girl who wants to train to be a geisha starts as an (1)_____ with another geisha. As a beginner, or *maiko* [maɪkoʊ], the girl begins years of training that require hard work and lots of (2)_____. Each *maiko* usually trains with an older geisha who is (3)_____ and no longer works. The older geisha is usually very (4)_____ with the young girl and makes her work very hard. As part of the training, the *maiko* must (5)_____ several different artistic skills as the main purpose of her training.

maiko

geisha

A Geisha in Kyoto

kimonos

3

Today, Kyoto, just like any large city in the world, is a very busy city with modern buildings and lots of traffic. But beneath the modern surface, Kyoto is an ancient city where a mysterious icon of old Japan can be found: the geisha. As a symbol of female beauty, the geisha continues to **fascinate**[1] the modern world. However, although the geisha is greatly admired, she is very rarely understood. Being a geisha is more than a job; it is a **calling**[2] which represents a traditional way of life.

This story is about a young woman named Umechika who is a *maiko*, a second-year apprentice. She is training hard in order to continue the ancient traditions of Japan. She has started her journey on the long road toward becoming a geisha.

---

[1] **fascinate:** interest greatly
[2] **calling:** a strong internal feeling that one should do something specific

 CD 2, Track 01

Becoming a geisha is far from easy. The extremely **rigorous**[3] training requires a lot of hard work and great discipline and Umechika is still adjusting to the changes. "When I first started," says Umechika, "there were many times that I was **scolded**[4] and I didn't even know why. Then I realized that this geisha world is so different from the world I used to know."

In order to become a geisha, Umechika had to leave her home, give up her real identity, her old life, and even her family. She had to start a completely new life. In order to achieve her dream, she decided to go to Kyoto, Japan's cultural heart and one of the last places where strict geisha training continues.

---

[3]**rigorous:** difficult; having high standards of behavior or action
[4]**scold:** tell someone in an angry way that he or she did something wrong

In Kyoto, the geishas usually live in certain parts of the city, and those are the only places where one can most often find them. Once in the city, Umechika had some difficulties in locating a place that would allow her to train as an apprentice. She was 19 years old already, and everyone said she was too old to start learning to become a geisha. But then she met Umeno, a retired geisha who runs a small teahouse. Umeno took one look at the young woman and decided that she had the face of a geisha. Umeno gave the 19-year-old girl a new name based on her own—and 'Umechika' was born.

Scan for Information

Scan pages 11 and 12 to find the information.

1. Why is having her hair styled so painful for Umechika?

2. Why is it difficult for her to sleep?

3. How long does it take to apply her make-up?

Becoming a geisha is not painless either. In fact, it's a long, exhausting path. For five years, Umechika must follow a very strict geisha routine. For example, every ten days she is required to go to a special hair salon to have her hair styled. The traditional *maiko* hairstyle looks very attractive, but it isn't easy to achieve or to maintain. While Umechika sits quietly in a chair, she has the the hairstylist twist and pull her hair into the *maiko* traditional style. The pressure of all this pulling is so strong that it produces a long-lasting **bald**[5] spot on Umechika's head. Then, in order to keep her hairstyle the way it is, she must sleep on a special hard pillow. It has been especially designed to maintain the shape of the hair, but it is so hard that it sometimes keeps her awake. However, it's more than just a traditional hairstyle that makes a geisha …

---

[5]**bald:** having no hair on one's head

Umechika's routine follows the same pattern every day and she has almost no time for herself. She spends half of her day in different classes, learning to dance, sing, and play instruments. She spends the other half of the day preparing for an evening of **entertaining**[6] clients. Entertaining them will include playing musical instruments, dancing, and serving drinks and food.

Before the evening begins, Umechika must go through the long process of applying the **elaborate**[7] traditional make-up that all geishas must wear. First, she must apply a white paste all over her face, neck, and shoulders. She must then paint on the detailed accents of the traditional geisha face, including a black line over the eye and bright red on the lips. Umechika's special make-up alone takes an hour and a half to apply.

Every day Umechika must transform the girl she is into a traditional icon of female beauty. It's exhausting and some girls can't take it, but that only encourages Umechika. "I have seen so many girls just quit, but that only strengthens my resolve," Umechika explains, "If I quit now, all those things I have put up with and worked so hard on would become meaningless." For this determined young woman, there's no turning back.

---

[6]**entertain:** host a group of people and keep them amused or interested
[7]**elaborate:** complicated

Getting dressed to meet clients also takes a very long time since geishas have to wear traditional Japanese clothes. It takes two women to dress Umechika in her beautiful *kimono* properly, Umeno and an assistant. Umeno is a businesswoman and Umechika is her most important investment, so Umeno needs to make sure that her apprentice meets the expectations of her clients. Umechika must look exactly right—perfect in fact.

Umeno's teahouse pays for all the young *maiko's* training, including hundreds of thousands of dollars for beautiful, expensive *kimonos* and **accessories**.[8] But in return, Umeno keeps all of Umechika's income. Umechika receives no pay and only receives two days off from work each month. Although this business arrangement may seem very hard on the apprentice geisha, in Japan it is considered a great opportunity. Becoming a geisha puts one on the path to a very high position in Japanese society.

---

[8]**accessory:** a small item of clothing, such as shoes, jewelry, etc.

What do you think?

1. How do you feel about Umechika's life?

2. Do you think the business arrangement with Umeno is fair to Umechika? Why or why not?

Later in the evening, the apprentices entertain at the teahouse. The businessmen who come there are some of the most powerful men in Japan. For them, the teahouse is a place which is very far from their everyday lives. They come to relax, discuss a little business, and calm down after a stressful day. They are there to eat, drink, have some conversation, and watch musical performances—all in the company of fascinating geishas.

Although it can make her nervous, this kind of evening is actually good training for Umechika. The men who come to the teahouse are usually much older than she is. It can be extremely difficult and demanding to keep them happy and amused for the entire evening. However, she must learn to do this well—and how to do it while remaining calm, reserved, and polite.

There are a great many misunderstandings about geishas, especially outside Japan. They are much more than just teahouse staff. A geisha is above all, an artist, and a person with a very high level of learning. The arts that a geisha masters include performing traditional dances and playing musical instruments. Geishas are also well-trained in the arts of conversation and literature. It is because of all this learning and artistic training that geishas have a high social status in Japan.

This sense of high social status also extends to the geisha's clients. Although they enjoy the geishas' traditional performances, simply being near a geisha often seems to be enough for some. Geishas represent a way of life that is very different from most people's everyday life. It's a life that is very much linked to Japan's past, a life that represents a kind of escape from reality. One client explains that being with a geisha can actually be educational. "These geisha represent something beyond my everyday world," he says, "To meet these extraordinary women is in a way a learning opportunity and a way to elevate myself to a **superior**[9] being."

---

[9]**superior:** better; above average

It's obvious that becoming a geisha involves an incredible amount of hard work and **sacrifice**.[10] Many outsiders wonder why any modern woman would want to follow this kind of life. They don't understand that being a geisha allows someone like Umechika to experience another world; one that would be impossible in normal life. "I can do things that a normal school girl can't do," Umechika explains, "For instance, I can go to see *kabuki* theatre in these clothes and go to expensive restaurants with clients. I can talk to people I can't meet normally— **dignitaries**[11] and **CEOs**[12] of major corporations."

---

[10]**sacrifice:** giving up of something valuable for a specific purpose

[11]**dignitary:** an official; an important person

[12]**CEO (Chief Executive Officer):** a high-level central position in a business

Umechika also often has the opportunity to perform in special festivals to show off her skills as a dancer. This way of life is the realization of her childhood dreams, but doesn't she sometimes wish that she could just be a normal girl again? "Of course, every once in a while, I wish that I could just be a normal girl," says Umechika, "but it's like once or twice a year. It is hard, but it is something that I really enjoy, and that's why I can **endure**[13] it."

---

[13] **endure:** bear; put up with

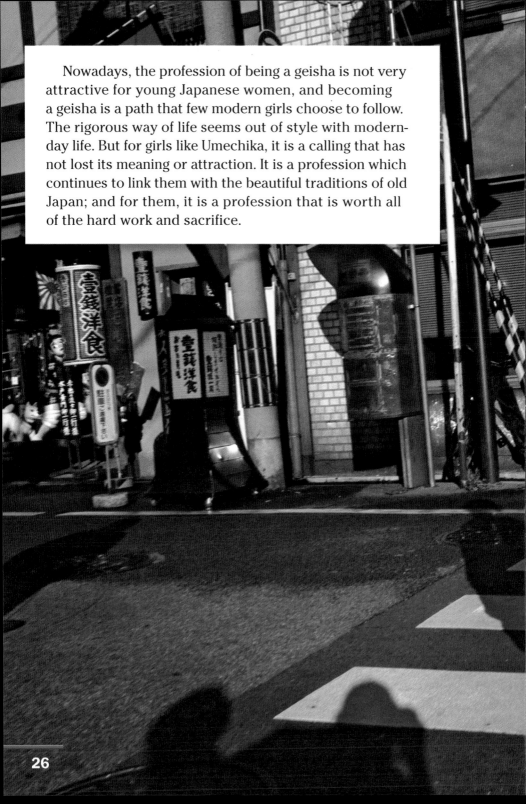

Nowadays, the profession of being a geisha is not very attractive for young Japanese women, and becoming a geisha is a path that few modern girls choose to follow. The rigorous way of life seems out of style with modern-day life. But for girls like Umechika, it is a calling that has not lost its meaning or attraction. It is a profession which continues to link them with the beautiful traditions of old Japan; and for them, it is a profession that is worth all of the hard work and sacrifice.

Summarize

Imagine that you are a reporter talking or writing about Umechika's life. What is her daily routine? Why has she chosen this lifestyle?

After You Read

1. Which of the following best summarizes the main point on page 4?
   A. Umechika doesn't want to be a geisha anymore.
   B. The geisha art form is disappearing in this century.
   C. Kyoto is a modern city that has many symbols of the traditional world.
   D. Japan's ancient traditions are in danger.

2. When she was scolded, Umechika became _____ the difference between her old world and the geisha world.
   A. known to
   B. angry about
   C. aware of
   D. frightened by

3. Why did Umechika have difficulty finding a place where she could train as an apprentice?
   A. She didn't have the face of a geisha.
   B. She didn't live in the geisha part of Kyoto.
   C. She was too stubborn.
   D. She was too old.

4. An appropriate heading for page 11 is:
   A. *Maiko* Life Full of Hard Moments
   B. Stress from Training Causes Bald Spot
   C. *Maiko* Knocked Down by Trainer
   D. Umechika Desperate to Sleep

5. Who applies Umechika's make–up to her face?
   A. Her trainer applies it for her.
   B. She goes to a make–up specialist.
   C. Umechika puts it on herself.
   D. This information is not found in the text.

6. On page 16, which word can be replaced by 'agreement'?
   A. investment
   B. expectation
   C. arrangement
   D. position

7. Why do geishas have a high social status in Japan?
   A. They perform for clients.
   B. They are well-trained in many areas of the arts.
   C. They work in teahouses.
   D. They are experts in ancient literature.

8. On page 21, what opinion is expressed by a geisha client?
   A. Geishas are Japanese goddesses.
   B. He can escape from business problems with a geisha.
   C. He enjoys traditional performances the most.
   D. Spending time with a geisha makes him a better person.

9. Which of the following people has Umechika met?
   A. a high-level businessman
   B. Umeno
   C. a dignitary
   D. all of the above

10. On page 24, to what does 'it' in 'it is something' refer?
    A. performing at special festivals
    B. realizing her childhood dreams
    C. wishing to be a normal girl
    D. living as a geisha

11. On page 27, which word can replace 'rigorous'?
    A. demanding
    B. gripping
    C. plentiful
    D. exclusive

12. What does the writer probably think will happen to Umechika?
    A. She will regret her decision to come to Kyoto.
    B. She will return to her previous identity and live in the modern world.
    C. She will graduate from being a *maiko* to a geisha.
    D. She will leave Umeno and work in another teahouse.

Inside Japan's
PERFORMING ARTS
an Interview with Benji Kato

Ms. Gura: Hello. I'm Aki Gura and welcome to our weekly program, Inside the Performance Arts. Today I'm pleased to introduce my TV viewers to a well-known expert in Japanese theater, Mr. Benji Kato. Mr. Kato, would you please describe *kabuki* to our audience?

Mr. Kato: *Kabuki* is a traditional form of Japanese theater that involves acting, singing, and dancing. It's also combined with colorful costumes and unusual techniques for telling a story on stage.

Ms. Gura: Is it similar to an American stage play or musical?

Mr. Kato: Not really. First of all, the tradition is about 400 years old and the movements of the actors are very stylized. They often move very slowly, almost as if they were in a dream. Also, the sound of the actors' voices is quite unusual. Their voices sound like a combination of singing and speaking.

Ms. Gura: That does sound very different! What does a play look like?

Mr. Kato: The actors often wear extraordinary and expensive *kimonos* and their faces are sometimes painted bright red or blue. This is done to help show what kind of people they are representing in the performance. And the stage itself is very unusual. Part of it is a long, narrow raised area that extends into the audience.

The Kabuki-za Theater in Tokyo offers daily performances.

Act		Performance Time	Tickets on Sale	Price (Yen)
1.	The Tale of Princess Usuyuki Act 1	11:00am – 12:25pm	10:30am	800¥
2.	The Tale of Princess Usuyuki Act 2	12:55pm - 1:45pm	12:35pm	1100¥
3.	The Tale of Princess Usuyuki Act 2	1:55pm - 3:15pm		
4.	The Niwaka Lion Dance	3:30pm - 3:45pm	3:00pm	600¥

When the actors use this part of the stage, they are surrounded by the audience. Another part of the stage actually moves around in a circle. This movement of the stage is used to create instant scene changes.

Ms. Gura: Wow! All of this in a 400-year-old tradition! Who are the actors?

Mr. Kato: *Kabuki* actors begin very young. They generally leave their families to study full-time with a master. It's almost like the training of a geisha. One very successful *kabuki* actor, Bando Tamasaburo, left home when he was seven. The actor who uses that name today is actually the fifth Bando Tamasaburo. The first actor to use this name lived hundreds of years ago. Each Tamasaburo trains his replacement and gives up the name when he retires. Today's Tamasaburo was born in 1950 and his real name is Shin-ichi Morita. He specializes in women's roles and appears on stages all over the world.

Ms. Gura: Wow! That's some interesting information. Thanks, Mr. Kato!

Mr. Kato: You're welcome. If you are interested in seeing a *kabuki* performance, there is a special series playing now at Tokyo's Kabuki-za Theater!

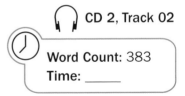

CD 2, Track 02

Word Count: 383
Time: _____

Vocabulary List

accessory (14)
apprentice (3, 4, 8, 14, 17)
bald (11)
calling (4, 27)
CEO (Chief Executive Officer) (23)
dignitary (23)
discipline (3, 7)
elaborate (12)
endure (24)
entertain (12, 17)
extraordinary (2, 21)
fascinate (4, 17)
geisha (2, 3, 4, 7, 8, 11, 12, 14, 17, 18, 21, 23, 27)
icon (2, 4, 12)
kabuki (2, 23)
kimono (2, 3, 14)
maiko (3, 4, 11, 14)
master (3, 18)
retired (3, 8)
rigorous (7, 27)
sacrifice (23, 27)
scold (7)
strict (3, 7, 11)
superior (21)